AF375226

Published by Enna's Press
ISBN: 979-8-9945835-3-1

Library of Congress Control Number: 2026903344

Art & Design: Created using licensed assets from Canva Pro.

For more books by the author, visit : iqralittlepages.com

JUVENILE NONFICTION / Concepts / General
JUVENILE NONFICTION / School & Education
JUVENILE NONFICTION / Social Themes / Emotions

Printed in USA. First Edition 2026.

Note to Parents & Educators

Dear Grown-ups,

Little ones experience big feelings long before they have words for them. This book helps toddlers like mine:

- Identify and name what they are feeling
- See emotions as normal and temporary
- Learn simple ways to respond when feelings feel big

Our gentle approach blends Montessori tools (like emotion cards and real-life photos) with the 4MAT learning cycle, guiding kids from *why* we have feelings to *how* to handle them.

Our little ones don't always have words for their big feelings. Sometimes they come out as meltdowns, sometimes as silence. I am still figuring this out; some days we nail it, other days we are both just trying to get through bedtime. This book is just something to hold onto, whenever it feels right.

Discover more books for curious toddlers : iqralittlepages.com
Happy Exploring and Growing together!

Author & Parent

For Yahya

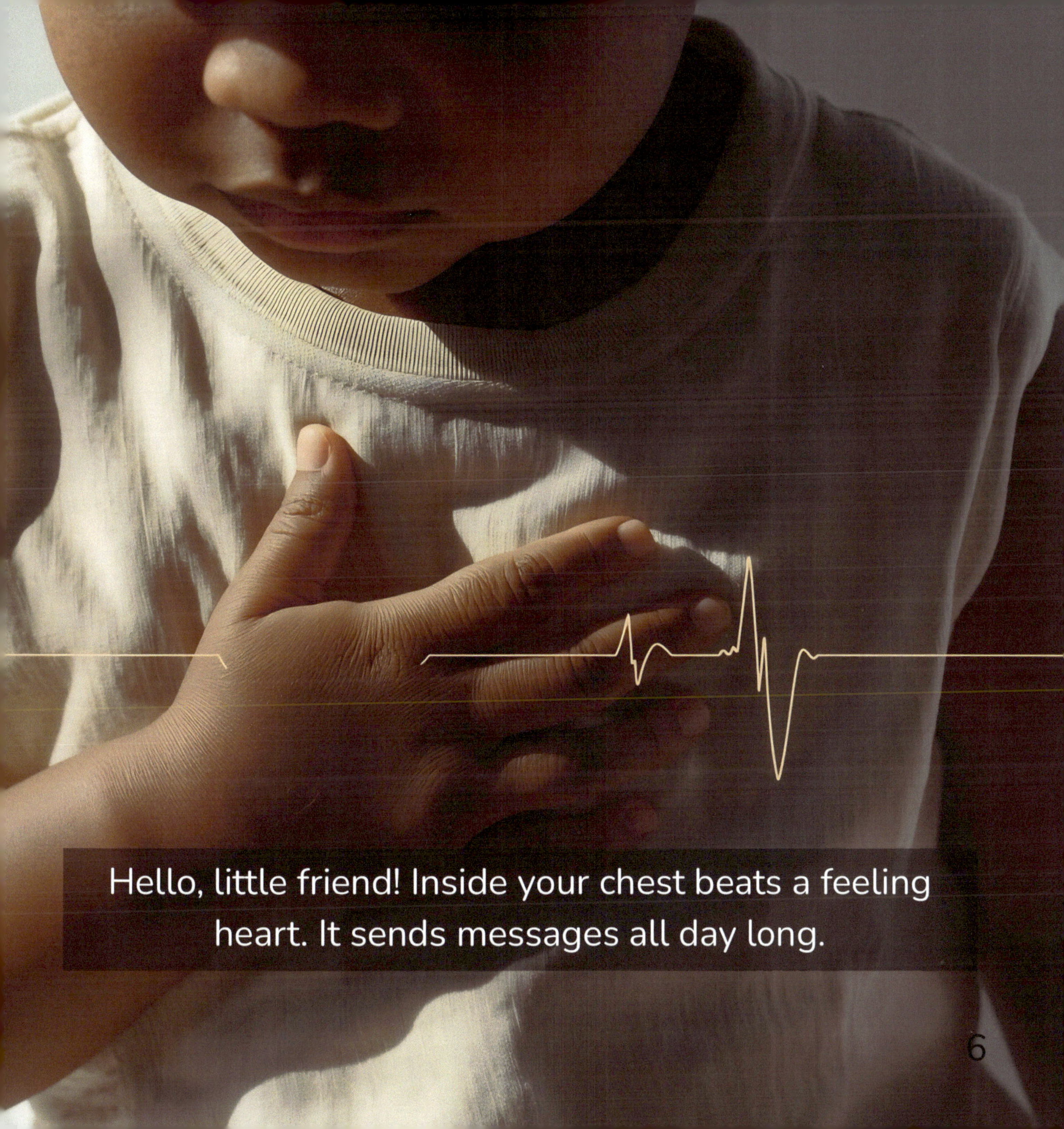

Hello, little friend! Inside your chest beats a feeling heart. It sends messages all day long.

6

Sometimes it feels light like a butterfly.
Sometimes it feels heavy like a rock.
Learning its language helps you understand yourself.
7

This is HAPPY.

Happy feels warm and sparkly. Your body want to wiggle, dance or share a hug!

This is SAD.

Sad feels quiet and slow. It's okay to feel sad. Comfort
helps your heart.

This is ANGRY.

Angry feels hot and tight. Our body wants to push and yell. We can learn gentle ways.

This is SCARED.

Scared makes our heart beat fast. It tells us to find safety or a helping hand.

This is CALM.

Calm feels like a soft blanket. Our breathing is slow.
Our mind is peaceful.

Feelings are visitors. We can welcome them, name them, and help them move on.

STEP 1: NAME IT. Point to your face and say:
'I feel HAPPY!' or 'I feel SAD.'

19

20

'I need a hug.'
hug?
Space please
'I need space'.
Grown-ups can help
your feeling heart.
STEP 3: ASK FOR HELP.
21

What if feelings had colors? Calm might be green like grass. Happy might be yellow like sunshine.

22

What if your friend's heart feels SAD? You could sit quietly together or share a toy. You are the helper of your own feeling heart.

LET'S PRACTICE! The Feeling Wheel &
Mirror Game

How to Play:
1) Make faces in the mirror!
2) Spin the wheel and show that feeling.
3) When big feelings come, remember: Name it, Breathe with it, Ask for help. You are learning your heart's language!